Hens, Fish, Moths

Written by Charlotte Raby
Illustrated by Laszlo Veres

Collins

ten red hens

a quick fox

ten red hens

a quick fox

a pink shell

a big fish

a pink shell

a big fish

bat wings

six moths

bat wings

six moths

/sh/

14

 Review: After reading

Use your assessment from hearing the children read to choose any GPCs and words that need additional practice.

Read 1: Decoding

- Ask the children to read pages 12 and 13. Ask them to point to the /ng/ sound and /th/ sound. (*wings, moths*)

- Look at the "I spy sounds" pages (14–15). Point to and sound out the sounds at the top of the pages. Ask the children to find as many things as they can in the picture that contain the /sh/ and /th/ sounds. (*fish, shells, shore, ship, sheep, shooting stars, shark fin, thread, moths, thimbles*)

Read 2: Vocabulary

- Go back over the three spreads and discuss the pictures. Encourage children to talk about details that stand out for them. Use a dialogic talk model to expand on their ideas and recast them in full sentences as naturally as possible.

- Work together to expand vocabulary by naming objects in the pictures that children do not know.

- On pages 8 and 9, ask the children: Which word describes the shell? (*pink*) Which words describes the fish? (*big*)

Read 3: Comprehension

- Reread page 3 and ask: What is special about the fox? (*it's quick*) Ask: What might it do quickly? (e.g. *jump, run, chase the hens*)

- Turn to pages 10 and 11, and ask questions about the objects. For example: Which animals have wings? (*moths, bats*)